WORDSTAR® PROFESSIONAL

THE POCKET REFERENCE

Chris Gilbert

Osborne **McGraw-Hill**
Berkeley, California

Osborne **McGraw-Hill**
2600 Tenth Street
Berkeley, California 94710
U.S.A.

For information on translations and book distributors outside of the U.S.A., please write to Osborne **McGraw-Hill** at the above address.

WordStar® Professional: The Pocket Reference

1234567890 DODO 898

ISBN 0-07-881402-2

Acquisitions Editor: Cindy Hudson
Copy Editor: Barbara Conway
Word Processor: Bonnie Bozorg
Proofreader: Kay Luthin
Production: Kevin Shafer, Peter Hancik

CONTENTS

INTRODUCTION

WordStar Professional: The Pocket Reference is a concise, comprehensive source of information on WordStar Professional versions 3.30, 3.31, 4.0, and 5.0. It is designed for the beginning, casual, or advanced user who is familiar with word processing and the basics of WordStar, but needs an accessible reference guide. This reference is organized into the following sections:

1. "WordStar Versions" discusses how to use this book with different versions of WordStar and how to convert a WordStar document from one version to another.

2. "Menus" describes the four ways of using WordStar, including the new pull-down menus of version 5.0.

3. "Messages" offers a list of the onscreen messages and prompts.

4. "Cursor Movement and Editing Commands" describes the commands for moving around WordStar and inserting and deleting text.

5. "Function Keys" discusses the 40 combinations of function keys and what they do.

6. "Functions and Features" is an alphabetical listing of features organized in the following manner:

- Feature name
- Subfeature
- CTRL (^) key commands
- Pull-down menu commands
- Function-key commands
- Characters displayed
- Description of the feature
- Cross-reference

WORDSTAR VERSIONS

How to Use This Book with Your Version of WordStar

Although this pocket reference addresses itself to WordStar versions 3.30, 3.31, 4.0, and 5.0, there are some differences in the way the commands are handled. When a feature has been added to a newer version, the version or versions are listed in parentheses after the feature heading.

For versions prior to version 5.0, all references to pull-down menus should be disregarded. For versions prior to version 4.0, references to function keys should be disregarded; function-key assignments are different in versions 3.30 and 3.31. There are only ten commands available, and they are all displayed on the screen for reference. Since versions 4.0 and 5.0 supply all 40 function-key combinations and WordStar does not display them all on the screen for reference, they are emphasized in this book.

Some WordStar operations are performed differently in different versions. For example, many commands in version 5.0 make use of *dialog* boxes and must be completed with F10. Older versions use the ENTER key. The differences will be listed, except for those previously noted.

How to Use Different Versions Of WordStar Documents

You can work on documents created on other versions of WordStar with three exceptions.

First, WordStar version 5.0 documents must be converted before being edited in previous versions. Converting a document will create a copy of the file that is then ready for editing in an earlier version. The original version 5.0 file will still remain as is. Here are the steps in the document conversion process:

1. At the Opening classic menu select Print a File. For the Opening pull-down menu, select F (File), then Print a File.

2. Type in the file name.

3. Select WS4 as the printer name.

4. At Redirect Output, type in a new file name for the copy.

5. Press F10 to convert.

Second, to use an older version of a personal dictionary in Wordstar version 5.0, sort the dictionary first. Open the dictionary (for example, PERSONAL.DCT) as a nondocument file, mark the entire file as a block, and use ^KZ to sort in ascending order. Save the file. (See the discussion of the Sorting feature for further information.)

Third, ruler lines from versions 4.0 and earlier may need adjustment in version 5.0. The newer version adjusts the ruler line to account for different-size fonts.

MENUS

There are four different ways to use WordStar Professional version 5.0. You can use pull-down menus (version 5.0 only), the original classic menus, CTRL key commands, and function keys. Each way, or interface, has a logic of its own. This choice of interfaces provides users with the most flexibility in learning and using WordStar. Casual users and newcomers can use WordStar in a way that is easy to learn and remember. More sophisticated users can use WordStar in more efficient and powerful ways.

Not all WordStar tasks are available with all interfaces. For example, you cannot change to the alternate pitch (12 pitch) with the function keys or the pull-down menus; you must use the classic menus or CTRL key commands.

Setting Help Levels and Changing Menus

To change from one interface to another, set the help level. The following table lists the interfaces, help levels, and command keys used to access each interface. The caret symbol (^) stands for the CTRL key.

Menu	Help Level	Associated Command Key
Classic menus		
No menus, no function-key labels	0	^
No menus	1	^
Edit menu off, submenus on	2	^
All menus on	3	^
Pull-down menus (Wordstar 5.0)	4	ALT
Function keys	All	F1 to F10
CTRL key commands	All	^

Note: CTRL key commands and function keys can be used at any help level, including pull-down menus.

To change help levels use ^JJ at help levels 0 through 3, and press ALT-O when using the pull-down menus (help level 4).

Classic Menus

The six classic menus offer the most complete access to WordStar. A series of submenus are accessed from the main Edit menu. Optionally, the Edit menu can be hidden to allow full-screen editing. The submenus are used for formatting (Onscreen Format menu), printing (Print Controls menu), and text manipulation (Edit, Quick Functions, and Block and Save menus). The Help menu offers further explanation of the tasks.

Note: The classic menus make extensive use of the CTRL key. On some newer-model computers, the positions on the keyboard of the CTRL key and the CAPS LOCK key have been switched; the CTRL key is located in the bottom row of the keyboard, near the spacebar instead of below the TAB key. A program called Switch, pro-vided with Wordstar versions 4.0 and 5.0, moves the functions of the CTRL key back to the home row (to CAPS LOCK, below the TAB key) for easy access.

To Change to Classic Menus from Pull-down Menus or No Menus Change the help level by pressing ALT-O from pull-down menus. To change to classic menus from help level 0 (no menu), use ^JJ.

To Use Classic Menus At the Edit menu hold down the CTRL (^) key and type the appropriate letter for one of the five submenus. For example, to set the left margin, access the Onscreen Format menu by using ^O. When the submenu screen appears (in this case, the Onscreen Format menu), type the letter of the command to perform. For example, type **L** to set the left margin. You do not need to hold down the CTRL key when in the submenu. Complete the command by answering any further prompts. In this example, typing **10** and pressing ENTER would set the left margin to 10.

Warning: Do not attempt to move the cursor or enter text while you are accessing a submenu; incorrect results will occur.

Wordstar always returns to the Edit menu after you use a submenu. To perform another command, access the correct submenu.

To Return to the Edit Menu from a Submenu Without Completing a Command You merely press the spacebar.

Note: It is not necessary to wait for a submenu to complete the keystrokes. See the discussion of CTRL key commands.

Pull-Down Menus

The pull-down menus are new to WordStar with version 5.0. For newcomers to WordStar, they offer a more coherent view of commands than the classic menus, and they are easier to learn and remember for casual users.

To Change to Pull-Down Menus from Classic Menus or from No Menu Change the help level with ^JJ to help level 4.

To Use Pull-Down Menus Hold down the ALT key, and then type the letter of the appropriate pull-down menu from the list at the top of the screen. For example, to set the left margin, access the Layout menu by holding down the ALT key and typing **L**. To perform a command, move the light-bar with the up and down arrow keys and press ENTER at the desired task. Complete the selection by answering any further prompts. In some cases, F10 is required to finish. To move to a neighboring pull-down menu, use the right or left cursor movement keys.

WordStar always exits a pull-down menu after you perform a task.

You may also press ALT-spacebar and then move the cursor along the top of the screen to access the pull-down menus.

To Exit a Pull-Down Menu Press the ESC key.

Function Keys

Function keys allow you to perform tasks with as little as one keystroke. The ten function keys, when combined with the SHIFT, CTRL, and ALT keys, offer 40 possible combinations. The default settings of the function keys are consistent with the standards of the personal computer software industry. For example, F1 accesses the Help menus. Although the function keys offer only a subset of all WordStar commands, they can be used interchangeably with pull-down menus and classic menus. Using WSChange, it is possible to customize the function-key combinations.

There is no need to set the help level to use function keys; they can be used at all help levels.

Warning: Do not attempt to use function keys while you are accessing a WordStar classic submenu; incorrect results may occur.

To Use Function Keys See the section "Function Keys" later in this reference for a complete list. In addition, function keys are displayed at the bottom of the screen when help levels 1 through 3 are used. A keyboard template also is included with WordStar.

CTRL Key Commands

CTRL key commands provide an efficient way to use WordStar, because they allow you to keep your hands on the home row of the keyboard; it is not necessary to reach for out-of-the- way function keys or cursor movement keys. (See the section "Cursor Movement and Editing Commands.") All operations of WordStar are available with the CTRL key commands.

To Use CTRL Key Commands The CTRL key commands can be used at all help levels. The keystrokes are the same as for classic menus; however, no submenu will appear.

MESSAGES

Status Line

- **Command** displays the current command in the top-left corner. For example, in the Onscreen menu, "O" is displayed.
- **Drive letter and file name.**
- **Wait** signifies that a lengthy command is in operation, such as Find/Replace or Go to Page.
- **P, L, C** shows the page, line, and column numbers. No pages are shown in Nondocument mode.

- **Insert** indicates that Insert mode is On. It disappears when Insert mode is Off.
- **Protect** shows that a file is protected and cannot be edited.
- **Align** is normally displayed to show that Auto-align is On. Text will wrap to the next line whenever the right margin is encountered.
- **Mar-Rel** indicates that Margin Release is On; no wordwrap will occur.
- **Preview** indicates that Preview is On. The file is viewed as it would print out; no editing is allowed.
- **LinSp** displays if line spacing is other than single space; for example, "LinSp-2".
- **Column** indicates Column mode.
- **ColRepl** indicates Column Replace.
- **Decimal** indicates that the TAB key has been pressed to a decimal tab. Numbers and text will line up right-justified or on the decimal point.
- **Replace? Y/N** asks whether to replace a word or not when Find/Replace is running.
- **Large-File** indicates that the current file does not fit entirely in memory. WordStar swaps parts of the file back and forth from the disk.

- **Dot-Limit** warns that the number of dot commands in the document is more than the number that can be kept track of during editing.
- **Printing** indicates that you are printing in the background while editing.
- **Print wait** indicates that you are printing in the background and printing is paused. Use ^KP while editing or type **P** or **M** at the Opening menu, and then type **C** to resume printing.
- **RgtJust** indicates that justification is on.
- **Auto-In**, in Nondocument mode only, shows when Auto-indent is On. To switch on and off, use ^6.

Flags

Flags are symbols located on the right side of the screen. They indicate the status of the line. The following table describes what a line contains when it has one of the following flags:

Flag	Contents
:	Dot command (affects printing only)
.	Dot command (affects onscreen format and printing)

Flag	Contents
1	Dot command (affects onscreen format and printing; best at top of page, line 1)
<	Carriage return
^	Bottom of document
(no character)	Soft return (wordwrap character)
?	Unfinished or incorrect dot command
P	Page break
+	Text extends beyond the right of the screen
F	Form feed (^PL)
-	Carriage return without line feed (^P-ENTER)
J	Line feed without carriage return (^PJ)

CURSOR MOVEMENT AND EDITING COMMANDS

Cursor Movement Commands

Use the following commands at the standard Edit menu or in pull-down menus. You cannot move the cursor when a WordStar submenu or pull-down menu is displayed. The CTRL key is represented with a ^.

Command	Cursor Movement
→, ^D	Right one character
←, ^S	Left one character
^ →, ^F	Right one word
^ ←, ^A	Left one word
↑ Up arrow, ^E	Up one line
↓ Down arrow, ^X	Down one line
^F10, ^QD	Right to end of line
^F9, ^QS	Left to end of line
TAB, ^I	Right to tab stop
HOME, ^QE	Up to top of screen
END, ^QX	Down to bottom of screen
^HOME, ^QR	To beginning of document
^END, ^QC	To end of document
^F4, ^QI	To page in document file
^QI	To line in nondocument file
^F4+*x*, ^F4-*x*, ^QI+*x*, ^QI-*x*	*x* number of pages forward or backward
^QG(character)	Forward to indicated character
^QH(character)	Backward to indicated character
^QB	To the beginning of a block marker
^QK	To the end of block marker
^Q0 through ^Q09	To marker 0 through 9
^QP	To previous cursor position

Command	Cursor Movement
^QV	To the last text found with ^QF

WordStar Diamond

It is possible to move the cursor without using the separate cursor movement keys on the side of the keyboard. Instead, use the CTRL key with the appropriate letter key listed in the previous table. This makes it possible to increase typing speed by keeping your hands on the main rows of the keyboard.

WordStar has organized the cursor movement keys in the form of a diamond, as follows:

```
                  Line up
                    ^E
Cursor left  ^S           ^D  Cursor right
                    ^X
                 Line down
```

To move the cursor a word to the right or left, or up or down a screen, use extensions of this format: ^F moves the cursor right one word, ^A moves the cursor left one word, ^R moves the cursor up one screen, ^C moves it down one screen.

Scrolling Commands

Command	Movement
^PGUP, ^W	Up one line
^PGDN, ^Z	Down one line
^PGUP, ^R	Up one screen
^PGDN, ^C	Down one screen
^QW	Up screen continuously
^QZ	Down screen continuously
Spacebar	Stop
0 through 9	Control speed (0 is fastest)

Delete Keys

Command	Text to Delete
^G or DEL	Character
^H or BACKSPACE	Previous character
^T, F6	Rest of word (beginning at cursor)
^G, ^T, DEL	Carriage return (place cursor at end of line)
^Y, F5	Line
^QY	Line to the right of cursor
^Q-DEL	Line to the left of cursor
^QT-character	From cursor to specific character
^QT-period	Sentence
^QT-ENTER	Paragraph

Commands	Text to Delete
Mark block ^KB and ^KK (see "Blocks"), ^KY, or SHIFT-F5	Block

The commands for deleting a character (^G), word (^T), and line (^Y) are grouped together on the keyboard for easier access.

Note: To restore deleted text use ^U (Unerase).

Insert Keys

Commands	Text to Insert
Type characters or words (Insert mode is on)	Character or word
spacebar (Insert on)	Space
ENTER (Insert on)	Line above cursor
^N	Line below cursor
Mark beginning and page end of block. Move cursor to new location. Use ^KV to move, ^KC to copy	Sentence, paragraph,

Commands	Text to Insert
^KR	Another file

FUNCTION KEYS

Key	Effect
F1	Displays Help menus
F2	Undoes or restores last deleted text
F3	Begins or ends underlining
F4	Begins or ends boldface
F5	Deletes line
F6	Deletes word
F7	Aligns paragraph
F8	Inserts the current ruler line
F9	Saves and continues editing document
F10	Saves and exits document
SHIFT-F1	Turns display off or on
SHIFT-F2	Centers the current line
SHIFT-F3	Checks the spelling for the rest of the file
SHIFT-F4	Checks the spelling of the current word
SHIFT-F5	Deletes a block
SHIFT-F6	Hides a block
SHIFT-F7	Moves a block
SHIFT-F8	Copies a block

Key	Effect
SHIFT-F9	Marks the beginning of a block
SHIFT-F10	Marks the end of a block
^F1	Finds text
^F2	Finds and replaces text
^F3	Finds text again
^F4	Goes to an indicated page
^F5	Sets left margin
^F6	Sets right margin
^F7	Sets paragraph margin
^F8	Places a page break
^F9	Moves cursor to the beginning of the line
^F10	Moves cursor to the end of the line
ALT-F1	Draws vertical graphics character
ALT-F2	Draws horizontal graphics character
ALT-F3	Draws top-left-corner graphics character
ALT-F4	Draws top-right-corner graphics character
ALT-F5	Draws bottom-left-corner graphics character
ALT-F6	Draws bottom-right-corner graphics character

Key	Effect
ALT-F7	Draws top "T" graphics character
ALT-F8	Draws bottom "T" graphics character
ALT-F9	Draws left "T" graphics character
ALT-F10	Draws right "T" graphics character

FUNCTIONS AND FEATURES

This section describes commonly used features of the WordStar program.

ADDITIONAL PROGRAMS/FEATURES

CTRL Key Commands Type **A** at the Opening menu, and select a program.

Select either MailList or Telmerge.

ALIGN PARAGRAPHS/TEXT

To Align Current Paragraph

CTRL Key Commands Place the cursor on the first line of the paragraph, and use ^B (Align).

Pull-Down Menu Press ALT-L for the Layout menu, and select Align Rest of Paragraph.

Function Key F7

To Align Paragraphs for the Rest of the File (Versions 4.0 and 5.0)

CTRL Key Commands ^QU (Quick menu, Align)

Pull-Down Menu Press ALT-L for the Layout menu, and select Align Rest of Document.

To Turn Auto-Align Off or On

CTRL Key Commands Use ^OA (Onscreen menu, Align)

To Align at Print Time

Dot Command .PF

Use Align after you have done any of the following:

- Added or deleted blocks of text

- Changed margins or tabs
- Turned justification off or on
- Used the Indent command
- Changed line spacing or fonts

This will reform a paragraph or document so that it matches the new settings.

Place the cursor on the first line of the text that is to be aligned. If the paragraph has been indented, use the Temporary Indent command (^OG) again before aligning the text. (See Indent.) Use ^QU to align an entire file from the cursor position. Press ESC to interrupt aligning.

With Auto-align set at On (the default setting), editing text will cause WordStar to realign a paragraph automatically. With Auto-align set at Off or with ^B or ^QU, text will not realign automatically.

To exclude specially formatted paragraphs, tables, or columns from being aligned when using either ^B or ^QU, use the dot command .AW *off* above the text and .AW *on* below it.

ANNOTATION

See Notes.

ASCII FILES

To Open an ASCII File from the Opening Menu

Classic Menu Type **N**, type the file name, and press ENTER.

Pull-Down Menu Type **F** for the File menu, and open a nondocument file.

To Change a WordStar File to an ASCII File

Classic Menu At the Opening menu type **P** (or while editing use ^KP). Type a new file name, or press ENTER to accept last file edited. Move the cursor down to "Name of Printer?" and type **ASCII**. To assign a different new file name, move to "Redirect Output to" and change the name. Press F10 to finish.

Pull-Down Menu At the Opening menu type **F** (or while editing press ALT-F) and select Print. Type a new file name, or press ENTER to accept last file edited. Move the cursor down to "Name of Printer?" and type **ASCII**. To assign a different new file name, move to "Redirect Output to" and change the name. Press F10 to finish.

To Create a Preview ASCII File (With Headers, Footers, and so on)

An ASCII file does not contain special WordStar formatting characters. Use ASCII files when you want to use a WordStar document in a spreadsheet or communications package or in another word processing program.

Converting a WordStar file requires the use of the Print command to print an ASCII version to the disk instead of to a printer. Converting a WordStar file to ASCII takes out the eighth bit (the formatting characters) and replaces soft returns in paragraphs with hard returns. The resulting file will not contain dot commands or printer codes.

To create an ASCII file that closely resembles what you would get if you printed on paper, including headers, footers, correct page breaks, and inserted data (for merge printing), type **PRVIEW** instead of ASCII in all the previously mentioned ASCII-file commands and menus.

AUTO-INDENT (VERSIONS 4.0 AND 5.0)

CTRL Key Commands ^6

For use with nondocument files only, Auto-indent will cause the left margin of each new line to match that of the line above. It is useful for using WordStar in structured programming.

To indent in Document mode, use the Temporary Indent command or change the left margin. (See also sections on Align Paragraphs and Word Wrap.)

When you use ^6, "Auto-In" appears in the status line. Use the TAB key, ^I, or the spacebar to move the cursor to the desired column. Type the first line and press the ENTER key. The next line will line up with the first. To turn off Auto-indent, repeat the command ^6.

BACKUP

WordStar keeps the previously saved version of a file in another file with the extension .BAK. To edit this file, rename it with another extension first. Use WS-Change to set Automatic Backup to On. (See Automatic Backup, Rename a File, Copy a File, and Save.)

Automatic Backup (Version 5.0)

This feature causes WordStar to back up the current document automatically. The default setting is Off. Use WSChange to set the duration (in seconds) before a backup is done after the last use of the keyboard. In WSChange select D (Wordstar), C (Other Features), G (Miscellaneous), I (Automatic Backup).

BIDIRECTIONAL PRINTING

Dot Command .BP on or .BP off

This dot command sets bidirectional printing. The default setting is On, which causes the printer to print in both directions. On some daisy-wheel printers you can turn it off to improve print quality. This dot command can be used anywhere in a file.

BINDING SPACES

CTRL Key Commands Use ^PO (Print menu, Binding Space).

Characters Displayed "^O"

A binding space keeps phrases such as dates and addresses from separating when they occur at the end of a line. Substitute a binding space for a space; "^O" will display instead. For example, May^O18,^O1987 will print as May 18, 1987.

BLOCKS (MARKING)

To Mark a Block of Text

CTRL Key Commands Move cursor to the beginning of the text and use ^KB (Block menu, Begin).

Move cursor after the end of the text and use ^KK (Block menu, End).

Pull-Down Menu Move cursor to the beginning of the text. Press ALT-E for the Edit menu and select Begin Block.

Move cursor to the end of the text. Press ALT-E for the Edit menu and select End Block.

Function Key Move cursor to the beginning of the text and press SHIFT-F9.

Move cursor to the end of the text. Press SHIFT-F10.

Mark a block of text to

- Copy text
- Move text
- Delete text
- Add numbers
- Save text to another file

A block can consist of characters, words, sentences, paragraphs, or pages. A column can be marked as a block when WordStar is in Column mode (^KN or ^KI). Only one block can be marked at a time.

The beginning of the block must be marked above or to the left of the end of the block. A block is highlighted when marked. When either the beginning or end marker is set without the other, the respective code, <B> or <K>, is displayed.

To Move the Beginning or End Marker

CTRL Key Commands Move cursor to the new po-sition and use ^KB or ^KK.

Pull-Down Menu Move cursor to the new position. Press ALT-E for the Edit menu, and select Begin Block or End Block.

Place the cursor in a new location and use ^KB or ^KK.

To Delete the Beginning or End Marker

CTRL Key Commands Place the cursor to the right of the marker and use ^KB or ^KK.

Characters Displayed <B> or <K>

Place the cursor to the right of B and use ^KB, or to the right of K and use ^KK.

Warning: If beginning <B> and end <K> markers show up at the same time on the screen, you have marked the block incorrectly. Remark the block.

BLOCK MATH (VERSIONS 4.0 AND 5.0)

CTRL Key Commands Move to the beginning of the numbers and use ^KB (Block menu, Begin).

Move after the numbers and use ^KK (Block menu, End) or ^KM (Block menu, Math).

Pull-Down Menu Move to beginning of the numbers. Press ALT- E for the Edit menu and then select Begin Block.

Move after the end of the numbers. Press ALT-E for the Edit menu and select End Block. Press ALT-O for the Other menu and select Block Math.

Function Key Move to the beginning of the numbers and press SHIFT-F9.

Move after the end of the numbers, press SHIFT-10. Use ^KM (Block menu, Math).

Block Math adds the numbers in a marked block. The answer is displayed at the top of the screen. To insert the answer at the cursor position use the shorthand command ESC= or use ESC$ for dollar format.

The following rules apply to using Block Math:

- A number is a set of digits surrounded by spaces or letters.
- Letters are not counted.

- A hyphen in front of a number is considered a minus sign.
- A number surrounded by parentheses is considered negative.
- A period immediately to the left of a number is considered a decimal point.
- A number can have no more than 30 digits.
- Answers have a maximum precision of 12 digits; above that, WordStar estimates the answer by using scientific notation; for example, 2e45 for 2 x 1045.
- Numbers in dot commands are ignored.

See also Math.

BOLD PRINT

CTRL Key Commands Move the cursor to the beginning of the text and use ^PB (Print menu, Bold).

Move the cursor after the end of the text and use ^PB.

Pull-Down Menu Move the cursor to the beginning of the text, and select ALT-S (Style menu).

Move the cursor after the end of the text, and select ALT-S (Style menu).

Function Key Move the cursor to the beginning of the text, and press F4.

Move the cursor after the end of the text, and then press F4.

Characters Displayed "^B"

Placed before and after text, this feature causes text to be printed darker. Text is highlighted on the screen.

Warning: If text is highlighted but does not print in bold, make sure you have installed the correct printer driver with WSChange.

CALCULATOR (MATH MENU)

See Block Math and Math.

CANCEL A COMMAND

CTRL Key Commands ^U

This feature stops a command and returns to the Edit menu. (See also Undo/Unerase.)

CASE CONVERSION (VERSIONS 4.0 AND 5.0)

CTRL Key Commands Move the cursor to the beginning of text, and use ^KB (Block menu, Begin).

Move the cursor after the end of the text, and use ^KK (Block menu, End). Use ^K", ^K', or ^K to mark the block. (Block menu, Upper/Lower/Sentence).

This command converts all letters in a block to uppercase, lowercase, or sentence case. With sentence case, the first letter of each sentence is converted to uppercase, the rest to lowercase. Release the CTRL key before pressing the punctuation after ^K.

CENTER

Center Current Line

CTRL Key Command Use ^OC (Onscreen menu, Center).

Pull-Down Menu Press ALT-L for the Layout menu and select Center Line.

Function Key SHIFT-F2

Use this command to center text after you have typed it. This will center one line at a time. Place the cursor anywhere on the line to be centered.

Center All Text That Follows

Dot Command .OC on or .OC off

This dot command centers all text that follows until .OC off is encountered. You must use the Align command to center any text that was entered before you use the dot command.

CHARACTER WIDTH

Dot Command .CW *n*, where *n* is the width in 1/120 inches. The default setting is *n* = 12 (12/120 inch), or 10 characters per inch.

This dot command changes the width of characters when printing, but it does not affect characters on the screen. Do not use this command for pitches of 10 or 12 characters per inch; use ^PN and ^PA for these. (See Pitch.) In version 5.0, do not use .CW with proportional fonts; use ^P= to select a font.

To change the character width, place the command above the text to be changed. The character width is limited, depending on your printer.

Changing the character width with .CW changes the width for the pitch that is currently in effect. It is possible to have two character widths in effect: one for the normal default pitch (^PN), and one for alternate pitch (^PA). Set one by using .CW after typing ^PN. Set the other by using a different .CW number after using ^PA. Switching between normal and alternate pitches will use the alternate character width settings. See Dot Commands.

COLOR PRINTING

CTRL Key Commands Move the cursor to the beginning of text to be printed and use ^PY (Print menu, Italics).

Move the cursor after the text to be printed and use ^PY.

Characters Displayed "^Y"

Use this commmand with printers with two-color ribbons. Place the command before and after the text for a second color. If italics are printed instead, install the correct printer with WSChange.

COLUMN MODE

CTRL Key Commands ^KN (Block menu, Column mode)

Pull-Down Menu Press ALT-E (Edit menu) and select Column Block mode.

Use before marking a column for moving, copying, or deleting.

COLUMN REPLACE (VERSIONS 4.0 AND 5.0)

CTRL Key Commands ^KI (Block menu, Column Replace)

Pull-Down Menu Press ALT-E (Edit menu) and select Column Replace mode.

Use with Column mode to copy over text when copying or moving a column, or to leave a blank "hole" when moving or deleting. When Column Replace is off, a column is inserted in *front* of existing text.

COLUMNS—NEWSPAPER-STYLE (VERSION 5.0)

Dot Command .CO *m, n*, where *m* represents the number of columns and *n* represents the number of spaces between columns. To space in inches, follow the variable *n* with ".

To Create a Column Break

Dot Command .CB

To Turn Off Columns

Dot Command .CO

Type this dot command at the beginning of a new page.

To Keep Lines Together in a Column

Dot Command .CC *n*, where *n* represents the number of lines to keep together.

▶ COMMENTS

Dot Command .. or .IG

These dot commands prevent comments from printing. Place them at the left side of the screen for each comment line. Comment lines may extend past the right margin; they will not be wrapped. (See Notes.)

▶ CONDITIONAL PAGE BREAK

Dot Command .CP *n*, where *n* represents the number of lines.

Use the Conditional Page Break command to keep a number of lines together on one page. This dot command is useful for preventing tables, charts, and paragraphs from being split across pages. (See Page Breaks.)

► CONTROL CODES AND THE CTRL KEY

WordStar control codes are special formatting characters that cause the printer to print italics, underlines, bold print, superscript, subscript, and other special characters. They are displayed on the screen when the onscreen display is turned on with ^OD. Control codes consist of the Control character (^) followed by a letter. For example, ^B is the control code that causes text to print in bold (darker) print. The control code is placed before and after the text. Control codes are deleted like any other character.

► CONVERT A DOCUMENT

See "WordStar Versions" at the front of the book.

► COPY FILE

Classic Menu At the Opening menu type O or while editing use ^KO (Block menu, Copy). Type in the file name to copy, and press ENTER. Type in the new file name and press ENTER.

Pull-Down Menu At the Opening menu type **F** for the File menu or while editing press ALT-F. Select Copy a File and press ENTER. Type in the file name to copy, then the new file name.

The Copy File commands make a copy under another name, or the same name on a different drive or directory. WordStar will prompt you for the name of the file to copy and then the new file name for the copy. If the new file name already exists, you will be prompted to "overwrite" it. Answer Y or N. The copied file will be located on the current drive and directory unless you specify otherwise; for instance, B:NEWFILE or B:\NEWDIR\NEWFILE.

► COPY TEXT

To Copy Text Within One File

CTRL **Key Commands** Move the cursor to the start of the text, and use ^KB (Block menu, Begin).

Move the cursor to the end of the text to be copied, and use ^KK (Block menu, End).

Move the cursor to a new location, and use ^KC (Block menu, Copy Text). Use ^KH (Block menu, Display) to stop the highlighting.

Pull-Down Menu Move the cursor to the beginning of the text. Press ALT-E for the Edit menu, and select Begin Block.

Move the cursor after the end of the text. Press ALT-E for the Edit menu and select End Block.

Move the cursor to a new location, press ALT-E, and select Copy Block. Press ALT-E and select Hide/Show Block.

Function Key Move the cursor to the text to be copied, and press SHIFT-F9 (Block Begin).

Move the cursor to the end of the text to be copied, and press SHIFT-F10 (Block End).

Move the cursor to a new location, and press SHIFT-F8 (Block Copy). Press SHIFT-F6 (Block Hide).

Use these commands to copy a block of text to a new location within the same file. To copy a column, turn on Column mode (and Column Replace, if desired) first. (See Blocks.)

▶ COUNT WORDS/CHARACTERS (VERSIONS 4.0 AND 5.0)

To Count Words and Characters In a Block of Text

CTRL **Key Commands** Move the cursor to the beginning of the text and use ^KB (Block menu, Begin).

Move the cursor to the end of the text, and use ^KK (Block menu, End). Use ^K? (Block menu, Count).

To Count Characters to the Cursor Position

CTRL **Key Commands** ^Q? for Quick menu, Count.

▶ CURSOR MOVEMENT

See the cursor movement table at the beginning of this book.

▶ CUSTOM PRINT CONTROLS

To Use Custom Print Controls

CTRL **Key Commands** Use ^PQ, ^PW, ^PE, or ^PR (Print menu).

These commands send codes to the printer to control special tasks such as italics, character font and size, and paper orientation. The tasks vary by printer. Turn on the custom print controls by placing the printer control code before the text. Turn them off with a second control after the text. The same code is usually not used to both turn on and turn off a task. Print a test file to determine what each custom print command does for your printer.

To Reset Custom Print Controls

Dot Command .XQ, .XW, .XE, or .XR

Change which codes are sent to the printer by using WSChange for all files, or use these dot commands for the current file only for versions 4.0 and 5.0.

The .X dot commands must be followed with the appropriate hexadecimal printer codes. These can be found in your printer manual. The following is an example of .X printer controls, which reset the ^PQ and ^PW printer controls to print condensed characters on an Epson-compatible printer:

```
.XQ 0F
.XW 10
^QThis sentence will be in condensed print.^W
```

CUT AND PASTE

See Move Text.

DATE (VERSIONS 4.0 AND 5.0)

Command Press ESC-@ or type **&@&**.

This command inserts today's date, based on the computer's system clock. An example of the default format is January 31, 1989. This format can be changed with WSChange.

Press ESC-@ to produce a static date that will not change. Type **&@&** to produce a dynamic date that will change to reflect the current date each time the file is printed (use Merge Print).

DECIMAL TABS

To Set a Decimal Tab in the Current Ruler Line

CTRL Key Commands Use ^OI #*n* (Onscreen menu, Set Tab), where *n* is the number of spaces.

Pull-Down Menu ALT-L, Margins and Tabs

To Insert New Ruler Line and Set Decimal Tabs

CTRL **Key Commands** Use ^OO (Onscreen, Insert Ruler Line). Move to the location in the ruler line. Use # for decimal tab.

These commands line up numbers by their decimal points and right-justify text. The following are examples of aligning numbers and text by a decimal tab:

```
        100
          1.3456
$4,235,123.12
           .33-
     longer
      short
```

To use a decimal tab, press the TAB key until the cursor is below the decimal tab stop and the word "decimal" appears in the status line. Type in the number or word; the characters are inserted to the left of the cursor. Decimal mode ends when you press the spacebar or type a decimal point (period), and the decimal indicator disappears from the status line. Characters typed at this point are inserted to the right of the cursor in the normal fashion.

If characters encounter another tab stop or a margin to the left, Decimal mode will be turned off. In this case, make more room for the numbers by deleting the tab stop or stops to the left or by moving the decimal tab to the right.

DELETE A FILE

CTRL Key Commands At the Opening menu type **Y** or while editing use ^KJ (Block menu, Delete File). Type in a file name and press ENTER. Type **Y** to confirm.

Pull-Down Menu At the Opening menu type **F** (File), or while editing press ALT-F for the File menu. Select Delete a File. Type in the file name and press ENTER. Type **Y** to confirm.

WordStar will prompt you for the name of the file to delete. If the file is located on a different drive or in a different directory, precede the name with the drive letter or path name; for example, B:NEWFILE or B:\NEWDIR\NEWFILE.

DELETE TEXT

To Delete by Character, Word, or Line

See the delete and insert keys in the "Cursor Movement and Editing Commands" section of this book.

To Delete a Block of Text

CTRL **Key Commands** Move the cursor to the beginning of the text, and use ^KB (Block menu, Begin).

Move the cursor after the end of the text, and use ^KK (Block menu, End).

Delete with ^KY (Block menu, Delete Text).

Pull-Down Menu Move the cursor to the beginning of the text, and press ALT-E for the Edit menu. Select Begin Block.

Move the cursor after the end of the text. Press ALT-E for the Edit menu, and select End Block. Press ALT-E and select Delete Block.

Function Key Move the cursor to the beginning of the text, and press SHIFT-F9.

Move the cursor after the end of the text, and press SHIFT-F10 (End Block). Press SHIFT-F5 (Delete Block).

Text deleted with these commands is recoverable with Unerase (^U) unless the block is larger than 500 characters. If it is, WordStar will display this message regarding the block: "Too large to undo later. Erase anyway (Y/N)?". To increase the size of the unerase buffer, use WSChange. To delete a column, turn on Column mode first.

DIRECTORY DISPLAY

Classic Menu Type **F** at the Opening menu.

This command turns File or Directory Display on and off. Optionally, type in wild-card characters to display a subset of the files. For example, to display only files with the .BAT extension type ***.BAT** and press ENTER. To restore the default view of files, turn the option off and on again. When asked for file view, type *.*. (See also Logged Disk Drive/Directory.)

DISPLAY CONTROL CHARACTERS

CTRL Key Commands Use ^OD (Onscreen menu, Display).

This command turns control codes off and on (that is, "^B" for Bold or "^S" for Underscore). Turn Display off to view the document without control characters.

DOCUMENT FILES

See Open a File.

DOT COMMANDS

Use dot commands to control the formatting and printing of documents. Dot commands must start in column one against the left side of the screen. Dot commands can generally be entered on any line in a document, although most are placed at the beginning of the file for correct formatting. Each dot command must be on a separate line. Lines that contain dot commands are not counted in character, line, or page counts and are not printed.

A dot command can be typed in either upper- or lowercase. Do not type text that is to be printed on the same line as a dot command; it will not print. The exceptions are headers and footers.

You can print a document with its dot commands by printing it as an ASCII file. (See Printing later in this book.)

DOT LEADERS

CTRL Key Commands ^P

This command inserts periods to the next tab stop and is useful for table of contents entries.

DOUBLE SPACE

See Line Spacing.

DOUBLE STRIKE

CTRL Key Commands Move the cursor to the start of the text, and use ^PD (Print menu, Double).

Move the cursor to end of text, and use ^PD (Print menu, Double).

Double Strike prints each letter twice to produce a darker print. The text will be highlighted on the screen. Double Strike is usually not as dark as bold text.

Characters Displayed "^D"

DRAWING (VERSIONS 4.0 AND 5.0)

Function Key ALT-F1 through ALT-F10

These ten function keys allow lines and boxes to be drawn on the screen and to be printed, depending on your printer. To avoid drawing a box from scratch, insert the file called BOX that is included with WordStar. Turn Insert mode off by pressing the INS key when typing within a box to avoid changing its shape.

To prevent the Align command from changing the shape of a box, use .AW *off* above the box and .AW *on* below. If you are printing with proportional spacing, use .PS *off* above the box and .PS *on* below to turn it off. Otherwise, the lines may print out unevenly.

EDIT A DOCUMENT

See Open a File in this section, as well as the earlier sections "Cursor Movement and Editing Commands" and "Function Keys."

ENDNOTE

See Notes.

EXIT FROM A DOCUMENT

See Save a File.

EXIT FROM A MENU

Classic Menu Press the spacebar.

Pull-Down Menu Press ESC.

EXTENDED CHARACTERS (VERSION 5.0)

CTRL Key Commands Use ^P0 (zero) (Print menu, Extended Chars).

Use extended characters for displaying and printing foreign characters. For printers that use IBM extended characters, type **0** (zero) at the Print Controls menu to display a list of extended characters.

If your printer does not print IBM extended characters, find the corresponding ASCII code in the printer manual and enter it in the text by holding down the ALT key and typing the code.

FILE NAMES

A file name consists of one to eight characters (letters or numbers) followed by an optional period and one to three characters; for example, FILENAME.123. Acceptable characters include numbers, letters, or any of the following: ~ ! @ # $ % ^ & ( ) - _ { } ' .

FIND/REPLACE TEXT

To Find Text

CTRL Key Commands Use the ^QF command (for Quick menu, Find). Then type in the text to find, and type in any options.

Pull-Down Menu Press ALT-G for the Goto menu, and select Find Text. Type in the text to find, and type in any options.

Function Key Press ^F1. Type in the text to find, and type in any options.

To Find Text Again

CTRL Key Commands ^L

Pull-Down Menu Press ALT-G for the Goto menu, and select Repeat Previous Find/Replace.

Function Key ^F3

To Replace Text

CTRL Key Commands Use the ^QA command (for Quick menu, Find/Replace). Type in the text to find and replace, and then type in any options. Type **Y** to replace, **N** to leave as is.

Pull-Down Menu Press ALT-G for the Goto menu, and select Find and Replace Text. Type in the text to find and replace, and type in any options. Type **Y** to replace, **N** to leave as is.

Function Key Press ^F2. Type in the text to find and replace, and then type in any options. Type **Y** to replace, **N** to leave as is.

You can find and/or replace up to 65 characters at a time. WordStar finds the first matching phrase starting at the current cursor position. If you want to replace text, a prompt will ask you to verify the replacement. Type **Y** to replace, **N** to leave as is.

To find or replace control characters such as Bold (^B), use ^PB when prompted for the text to find. To find carriage returns, use ^PM^PJ.

Use ? as a wild-card character; for example, if you type **c?t** WordStar will find "cat", "cot", "cit", and "cut".

To find and delete text, use ^Y for Replace.

Use any combination of the following options:

Option	Action
W	Finds whole words only
U	Ignores case of text
B	Searches backwards

Option	Action
n	Searches for the *n*th occurrence of the text or replaces *n* number of times
G	Searches from beginning of a file
R	Searches through the rest of a file
N	Replaces text without asking
A	Aligns paragraph after replacing text (use .AW *off* to skip tables)
M	Replaces text using case of text found
?	Wild-card character

To set the default options, use WSChange.

To speed up the process of replacing text, press the spacebar after starting in order to turn off the display of replacements.

Warning: To be safe, save your file before large-scale replacements. If mistakes are made you can abandon them and open the original file.

FONTS (VERSION 5.0)

CTRL Key Commands Use ^P= (Print menu, Font).

Pull-Down Menu Press ALT-S for the Style menu, and select Choose Font.

This feature displays fonts available for the current printer. To display fonts for other installed printers, use ^P? first. A new font affects existing text only after you edit or align it (with ^B or ^QU). To customize fonts, use the program PRChange. Use this command for all proportional printing in version 5.0.

FOOTER

Dot Command Use .FO or .F1 for the first footer line, .F2 for the second footer line, and .F3 for the third footer line.

Pull-Down Menu Press ALT-L for the Layout menu, and select Footer.

Footer lines appear at the bottom of each page of a document when printed. There can be a maximum of three footer lines. Place the footer at the top of the first page that will contain the footer. To skip pages, disable the previous footer with .FO alone and place new footer lines at the top of a following page. Place the footer dot commands in column 1 with the footer text following on the same line. To include an automatic page number, type # anywhere on the footer line.

Here is a sample footer:

```
.F1 ABC Company, Inc.                    Page: #
```

To print on odd or even pages, only use .FOO, .F2O, .F3O, or .FOE, .F2E, .F3E.

FOOTNOTES (VERSION 5.0)

See Notes.

GRAPHICS (VERSION 5.0)

CTRL Key Commands Use the ^P* command (for Print Controls menu, Graphics).

Using this command, insert the name of an INSET PIX graphics file that will be printed with the document.

HEADERS

Dot Command Use .HE or .H1 for the first header line, .H2 for the second header line, and .H3 for the third header line.

Pull-Down Menu Press ALT-L for the Layout menu, and select Header.

Header lines appear at the top of each page of a document when printed. You can have a maximum of three header lines. Place the header at the top of the first page that will contain the header. To skip pages, place header lines at the top of a following page. Place the dot commands against the left side of the screen with the header text following on the same line. To include an automatic page number, type # anywhere on the header line. You may need to disable automatic page numbering with a blank footer (.FO) first.

Here is a sample header line:

```
.H1   ABC Company, Inc.                    Page: #
```

To print on only odd or even pages, use .HEO, .H2O, .H3O, or .HEE, .H2E, .H3E.

► HELP

CTRL Key Commands ^J

Function Key F1

Help levels are context sensitive; pressing F1 or using ^J displays a menu that pertains to the current task at hand.

► HELP LEVEL (CHANGE)

Classic Menu Use ^JJ (Help menu, help level).

Pull-Down Menu Press ALT-O for Other menu.

In these commands type **0** through **4** for the desired help level. (See the discussion of help levels in the "Menus" section of this book.)

HYPHENATION (AUTOMATIC)

To Turn Off Hyphenation for the Current Paragraph (Version 4.0)

CTRL Key Commands ^U

To Turn Hyphenation Off or On For the Current File

CTRL Key Commands Use the commands ^OH off or ^OH on (Onscreen menu, hyphenation).

For versions 3.30, 3.31, and 4.0 when hyphenation is on, the cursor stops on a word when it comes at the end of the line, extends past the right margin, and is larger than five characters. To hyphenate the word, type - (the hyphen key or dash). Optionally, move the cursor to a different hyphenation point first. You cannot move the cursor beyond the word or to the right of the right margin. To skip hyphenation and wrap the word to the next line, use ^B. To turn off hyphenation temporarily for the rest of the paragraph, use ^U.

For version 5.0, WordStar automatically inserts a "soft" hyphen when hyphenation is on. To hyphenate a word differently, type ^OE at the desired point.

To turn off hyphenation until the document is saved, use ^OH. When hyphenation is off, WordStar automatically wraps the word to the next line when it is too long for the right margin.

To permanently turn hyphenation off, use WSChange. Also use WSChange to change the default setting for the minimum number of characters required in a word for hyphenation.

INDENT A PARAGRAPH (TEMPORARY INDENT)

CTRL Key Commands Use ^OG (Onscreen menu, Temporary Indent).

Temporary Indent changes the left margin for a single paragraph at a time; only the next paragraph edited or aligned will be affected. After you type or align the paragraph, the original left margin setting will be restored.

To set Temporary Indent, use ^OG until the indent symbol (V) moves to the correct tab stop in the ruler line at the top of the screen. For example, typing ^OG five times will cause the temporary indent to be placed below the fifth tab stop. To place the indent at a column other than a current tab stop, set a new tab stop in the ruler line.

To edit an already indented paragraph, use ^OG again before editing text or aligning it. (See Margins for more permanent ways of indenting paragraphs.)

INDEXING

Indexing extracts an alphabetical listing of phrases, along with associated page numbers, from a document.

To Create Index Entries

CTRL Key Commands Move to the start of a phrase to mark and use ^PK (Print menu, Indexing). Move to the end of the phrase and repeat ^PK. Or use ^ONI (Onscreen, Index entry) and manually type *entry, sub-entry.*

Pull-Down Menu ALT-O (Other, Index entry) and enter *entry, subentry.*

Dot Command .IX *entry, subentry*

The longest index entry is 50 characters. ^PK marks existing phrases as entries. ^ONI and ALT-O will create new entries that can be hidden with ^OD for viewing. .IX also creates new entries.

To include subentries, separate with a comma. To mark the associated page number as bold, precede an entry with a + symbol. To omit the page number for cross-index entries, precede with a - symbol. To edit an entry, use ^OND.

To Create the Index (from Opening Menu)

Classic Menu I (Index), type the document name, and change any options. Press F10 to index.

Pull-Down Menu O (Other), I (Index), type the document name, and change any options. Press F10 to index.

WordStar creates a new file with the same file name as the document indexed, but with .IDX as the extension. Edit and print this file as the index.

You have the option to index every word in the document, except those listed in exclusion files—WSINDEX.XCL—and a custom file with the same name as the document file and the extension .XCL. In addition, you can select certain pages to be indexed.

▶ INSERT FILE

CTRL Key Commands Type the command ^KR for Block menu, Read, and type in the file name to insert.

This command inserts a file at the cursor position. If the file is a Lotus 1-2-3, Symphony, or Quattro spreadsheet, WordStar will prompt for a range or range name. Press ENTER to insert the entire spreadsheet.

INSERT MODE

Command INS key

This key turns Insert mode off and on. "Insert" appears at the top of the screen when this mode is on. When it is off, characters are typed over existing characters in text. (See the discussion of insert keys in the "Cursor Movement and Editing Commands" section of this book.)

INSERT TEXT

See the "Cursor Movement and Editing Commands" section of this book.

ITALICS

CTRL Key Commands Move the cursor to the beginning of the text, and use ^PY (Print menu, Italics).

Move the cursor to the end of the text, and use ^PY.

Pull-Down Menu Move the cursor to the start of the text to be italicized, press ALT-S for the Style menu, and select Italics.

Move the cursor to the end of the text, press ALT-S for the Style menu, and select Italics.

Characters Displayed "^Y"

This feature prints text in italics. The text will be highlighted on the screen. Some printers may not print italics. Place the printer control codes before the text to turn italics on and after the text to turn it off.

JUSTIFY

To Turn Justification On or Off Until File Is Saved (Versions 3.30, 3.31, and 4.0)

CTRL Key Commands Use ^OJ (Onscreen menu, Justify).

Justification causes the right margin of a paragraph to line up evenly. When Justify is off, a paragraph's margin is ragged. The default setting in WordStar is Justify on. When Justify is on, the status line displays the message "RgtJust."

To justify or unjustify text, turn Justify on or off, and enter text. For text that has already been entered use the

Align command (^B or ^QU) to realign the text according to the new setting.

The ^OJ command causes Justify to be on or off as long as you are editing a file. The default setting is restored when you exit.

To Store Justification Setting in a File for Version 5.0

CTRL Key Commands Use ^OJ (Onscreen menu, Justify).

Dot Command .OJ on or .OJ off

Use the .OJ on or .OJ off dot command to permanently set justification within a file.

LEFT MARGIN

See Margins.

LETTER QUALITY (VERSIONS 4.0 AND 5.0)

Dot Command .LQ on, .LQ off, or .LQ dis

This dot command instructs dot matrix printers to print in a higher-quality print style. The default setting is dis for discretionary. The fonts used determine whether LQ is on or off.

LINE HEIGHT

Dot Command .LH *n*, where *n* is in units of 1/48 inch.

Line Height is useful for changing the line spacing of text (during printing) without having to reformat the document on the screen. Text on the screen will not change, except for page breaks. To adjust the line spacing on the screen as well, use Line Spacing (^OS).

The default setting of Line Height is *n* = 8 (8/48 inch), or 6 lines per inch. Useful settings are

.LH 16	(double-spacing)
.LH 12	(1 1/2-spacing)

Decrease the Line Height setting to increase the number of lines per page. You may have to change Page Length to compensate.

LINE NUMBERING (VERSION 5.0)

Dot Command .L# *xy,z* (default = p1,3)

This feature prints line numbers in the left margin, creating legal pleading paper. If typed in the middle of a page, it takes effect on the following page. For *x*, type **p** to restart numbering at each new page or type **d** for continuous numbering. For *y*, type **1** for single-spacing and type **2** for double-spacing. With *z*, set the line-numbering column. If the page offset (.PO) does not leave enough room at print-time, WordStar will adjust it.

To Turn Off Line Numbering

Dot Command .L#0

If placed in the middle of a page, this command takes effect with the next full page.

► LINE SPACING

CTRL Key Commands Use ^OS *n* (Onscreen menu, Spacing), where *n* is the line spacing from 1 to 9.

Pull-Down Menu ALT-L, Margins and Tabs. Move to Line Spacing and type in number.

This command changes spacing between lines both on the screen and when printing. To change the line spacing for existing paragraphs, use ^B to align the current paragraph or ^QU to align the rest of the document. Reset temporary indents beforehand with ^OG, if necessary. (To change the line spacing at print-time without changing it on the screen, or to change it in fractions of an inch, see Line Height.)

LOGGED DISK DRIVE/DIRECTORY (CHANGE)

CTRL **Key Commands** At the Opening menu type **L**, or while editing use ^KL (Block menu, Change Drive/Dir).

Pull-Down Menu At the Opening menu type **F** (File) or while editing, use ALT-F, Change Drive/Directory)

Use this function to change to a different directory and/or disk drive. After the logged disk drive or directory is changed, all files that are created, copied, deleted, renamed, or written will exist in the new directory or disk drive. The current file, however, will continue to be saved to the original drive and directory.

MACROS

See Shorthand.

MARGINS

Margins are set in either inches or columns in version 5.0; for columns, use dot commands. Previous versions use columns only.

To Reset the Left Margin

CTRL Key Commands Use ^OL *n* (the Onscreen menu, Left), where *n* equals the new setting in inches. Press F10 to complete. The default setting is *n* = .00 inches.

Pull-Down Menu Press ALT-L for the Layout menu, and select Margins and Tabs. Type the new setting in inches. Press F10.

Function Key ^F5, type in the setting.

Dot Command .LM *n* or *n*" or +*n*"

Left margins are shown in the ruler line as L.

Use the dot command to set in columns or inches. Use ^B or ^QU to realign existing paragraphs to the new left margin.

To Permanently Store the Left Margin Setting in the Document (Version 4.0)

Dot Command Use .LM *n*, where *n* equals number of columns. The default setting is *n* = 0.

Text entered below the dot command will conform to the new margin. For existing text, use ^B or ^QU to realign paragraphs to the new margin.

To Reset the Left Margin for the Current Session Only (Versions 3.30, 3.31, and 4.0)

CTRL Key Commands Use ^OL (Onscreen menu, Left). Type in the new setting in columns, and press ENTER.

Press ESC without a column number to set the margin at the current cursor position.

To Reset the Left Margin at Print-Time (Page Offset) (Versions 3.30, 3.31, and 4.0)

Dot Command Use .PO *n*, where *n* equals number of inches. The default setting is *n* = 8 columns.

To Reset the Left Margin at Print-Time (Page Offset) (Version 5.0)

Pull-Down Menu ALT-L (Layout), Margins and Tabs. Move to Even page offset or Odd page offset. Enter the setting in inches and press F10.

Dot Command .PO *n* or *n*"; .POE *n* or *n*"; .POO *n* or *n*"

Page Offset controls the space between the left edge of the paper and the text at print-time. It does not alter text on the screen. This is the easiest way to change the left margin when printing, although the right margin will change as well. Place the dot command at the beginning of the file.

To Reset the Right Margin for the Current Session Only (Version 5.0)

CTRL Key Commands Use ^OR *n* (Onscreen menu, Right), where *n* equals number of inches. Type in the new setting in inches, and press F10. The default setting is *n* = 6.50 inches (column 65 at 10 pitch, column 78 at 12 pitch).

Function Key ^F6, type setting

Use the dot command .PO to set in columns or inches. Use ^B or ^QU to realign existing paragraphs to the new right margin.

To Permanently Store the Right Margin Setting in the Document (Version 4.0)

Dot Command Use .RM *n*, where *n* equals number of columns. The default setting is *n* = 65.

Use ^B or ^QU to realign paragraphs to the new margin settings.

To Reset the Right Margin for the Current Session Only (Versions 3.30, 3.31, and 4.0)

CTRL Key Commands Use ^OR (Onscreen menu, Right). Type in the new setting in columns, and press ENTER.

Press ESC without a column number to set the margin at the current cursor position.

To Reset the Top Margin

Dot Command Use .MT *n*, where *n* equals number of lines. The default setting is *n* = three lines. For version 5.0, use *n*" for inches.

Pull-Down Menu For version 5.0, press ALT-L for the Layout menu, and select Margins and Tabs. Move to Top and type the new setting in inches.

The top margin controls the amount of blank space between the text and the top of a page when it prints. The top margin is not displayed on the screen. Page breaks will change, however, as the top margin is changed (see Page Break). To fit more text on a page, decrease the number of lines in the top margin.

To Reset the Bottom Margin

Dot Command Use .MB *n*, where *n* equals number of lines. The default setting is *n* = eight lines. For version 5.0, use *n*" for inches.

Pull-Down Menu For version 5.0, press ALT-L for the Layout menu, and select Margins and Tabs. Move to Bottom and type the number of inches. Press F10.

The bottom margin controls the amount of blank space between the text and the bottom of a page when it prints. The bottom margin is not displayed on the screen. Page breaks will change, however, as the bottom margin is changed (see Page Break). To fit more text on a page, decrease the number of lines in the bottom margin.

To Reset the Header Margin

Dot Command Use .HM *n*, where *n* equals number of inches. The default setting is *n* = two lines. For version 5.0, use *n*" for inches.

Pull-Down Menu Press ALT-L for the Layout menu, and select Margins and Tabs. Move to Header and type in the number of inches. Press F10.

The header margin is the space between the text and the header when a document prints. Place the dot command at the top of the first page.

To print a header of two or three lines, increase the header margin by the same number of lines.

To Reset the Footer Margin

Dot Command Use .FM *n*, where *n* equals number of lines. The default setting is *n* = two lines. For version 5.0, use *n*" for inches.

Pull-Down Menu For version 5.0, press ALT-L for the Layout menu, and select Margins and Tabs. Move to Footer and type the new setting in inches. Press F10.

The footer margin is the space between the text and the footer when a document prints. Place the dot command at the top of the first page.

If you use a footer margin of 0, turn page numbering off (.OP).

To Set or Reset the Paragraph Margin (Versions 4.0 and 5.0)

Dot Command Use .PM *n*. For version 5.0, use *n*" for inches.

Pull-Down Menu For version 5.0, press ALT-L for the Layout menu, and select Margins and Tabs. Move to Paragraph and type the new setting in inches. Press F10.

The paragraph margin treats the left margin of the first line of a paragraph separately from the left margin of the rest of the paragraph. Use it to either indent the first line or indent the body of the paragraph.

To indent the first line of each paragraph, set the paragraph margin number larger than the left margin number. To indent the body of the paragraph and leave the first line to the left (hanging indent), set the paragraph margin to a number that is smaller than the left margin number.

To set a paragraph margin, type anywhere in the document but above the text to be affected. New text entered below the dot command will conform to the margin. Use ^B or ^QU to realign existing paragraphs. To turn off the paragraph margin, use .PM or .PM0.

To Store the Ruler Line in a Document (Versions 4.0 and 5.0)

CTRL Key Commands ^OO (Onscreen, Ruler)

Dot Command .RR

Function Key F8

To Release Margins

CTRL Key Commands Use ^OX (Onscreen menu, Release).

Pull-Down Menu ALT-L, Margin Release

► MATH (VERSIONS 4.0 AND 5.0)

CTRL Key Commands Use ^QM (for Quick menu, Math), and type in the formula.

Pull-Down Menu Press ALT-O for the Other menu, and type in the formula.

Use the Math Menu to perform calculations of mathematical functions, including logarithms, square roots, and trigonometric functions. Formulas and results can be inserted in a document, printed, or stored for later use.

The following are examples of formulas that can be calculated by using the Math menu:

```
2*3*4
8.5/12
2^2
sin(35)
sqr(4.35)
(5.123+137.36-1484.34)/6.3
```

Formulas are calculated in the following order:

1. Functions, that is, sin(), sqrt()
2. Exponentiation (^)
3. Multiplication, Division (*, /)
4. Addition, Subtraction (+, -)

Within each level, formulas are calculated left to right. Parentheses can be used to change the order of calculation. For example, in the last equation in the previous list of examples, the parentheses cause the division to be performed last.

The result of the calculation can be inserted into the document with the shorthand command ESC= or ESC$ for dollar format (see Shorthand).

See also Block Math.

MERGE PRINTING

To Merge and Print Files at the Opening Menu

Classic Menu Type **M** (Merge Print), and type in the master document name. Answer options, if appropriate, and then press F10.

Pull-Down Menu Type **F** and select Merge Print a File. Answer options, if appropriate, and then press F10.

To Merge and Print Files While Editing

CTRL Key Commands Use ^KP (Block menu, Print) and type **M** (Merge Print). Type in the master document name. Answer options, if appropriate, and press F10.

Pull-Down Menu Press ALT-F for the File menu, and select Merge Print a File. Answer options, if appropriate, and then press F10.

Two or more files can be merged at print-time. Optionally, data can be entered from the keyboard while printing. Merge Printing is useful for combining a standard document with variable information such as names and addresses to produce form letters, labels, envelopes, lists. Other uses include merging files to combine chapters of a book and prompting the user to enter data while printing.

To Insert Merge Dot Dommands

Dot Command Use .DF to read a data file and .RV to read variables.

To Insert Merge Variable Names

Commands

&var&	Prints data
&#&	Prints a page number
&_&	Prints a line number
&@&	Prints the date
&!&	Prints the time
&var/o&	Omits blank lines
&var/f&	Uses format F as defined with .SV

Usually, merge printing consists of a master document and a data file. This form letter is an example of a master document:

```
.df datafile
.rv name, address1, address2, greeting

&name&
&address1/o&
&address2/o&
```

Dear &greeting&,

(body of text)

.pa

Here is an example of a data file:

```
Don Johns, 30 W. Holly, "L.A., CA  94117",Don
Fred Johns, 23 Sunset, "L.A., CA  94117",Fred
Sally Suthe, 44 E. St., "L.A., CA  94117", Sally
```

Note: Each person's data must be on one line.

The variable names in the .RV (Read Variable) line in the master document are arbitrary names that will be assigned to the data in the data file. Each field between commas in the data file is matched to a different variable name in the .RV line in the master document. For example, Don Johns is matched to the variable *name,* and 30 W. Holly is matched to the variable *address1*.

Variable names can be placed anywhere in the master document below the merge dot commands, and can be repeated in different locations.

Quotes around the addresses prevent WordStar from reading the commas between city and state as variable delimiters.

To Insert Optional Merge Dot Commands

Dot Commands

.SV	Sets variable or format
.AV	Asks for variable
.DM	Displays message when printing
.CS	Clears screen and displays message
.FI	Inserts file at print time
.MA	Sets variable to math result

To Insert Conditional Merge Dot Commands

Dot Commands

.IF	Test condition
.EL	Does if condition is true
.EI	Ends if condition
.GO	Goes to top or bottom of document
.PF off or	
.PF on	Aligns paragraphs when printing
.PF dis	Aligns only paragraphs with variables

▶ MICROJUSTIFICATION

Dot Command Use .UJ on, .UJ off, or .UJ dis.

This command causes printers to space more evenly between words (and for some printers, between letters) when printing right-justified text. The .UJ dis command instructs WordStar to turn Microjustification off if your printer microjustifies too slowly. The default setting is .UF dis.

MOVE TEXT

To Move Text Within a File

CTRL Key Commands Move the cursor to the beginning of the text, and use ^KB (Block menu, Begin).

Move the cursor to the end of the text, and use ^KK (Block menu, End).

Move the cursor to a new location, and use ^KV (Block menu, Move) and ^KH (Block menu, Display).

Pull-Down Menu Move the cursor to the start of text to be moved, press ALT-E for the Edit menu, and select Begin Block.

Move the cursor after the end of the text, press ALT-E, and select End Block.

Move the cursor to the new location, press ALT-E, and select Move Block. Press ALT-E and select Hide/Show Block.

Function Key Move the cursor to the start of the text to be moved, and press SHIFT-F9.

Move the cursor to the end of the text, and press SHIFT-F10.

Move the cursor to the new location, and press SHIFT-F7 (Block Move) and SHIFT-F6 (Hide Shading).

These commands move a block of text to a new location within the same file (see Blocks). To move a column, use Column mode before marking text. Optionally, use Column Replace as well.

To Move Text from One File to Another Between Windows (Version 5.0)

CTRL Key Commands Move the cursor to the beginning of the text to be moved, and use ^KB (Block menu, Begin).

Move the cursor to the end of text, and use ^KK (Block menu, End).

Move to the second file with ^OK (Onscreen, Switch Window).

Move the cursor to the new location, and use ^KG (Block menu, Move Between) and ^KH (Block menu, Display).

Pull-Down Menu Move the cursor to the start of the text to be moved, press ALT-E for the Edit menu, and select Begin Block.

Move the cursor after the end of the text, press ALT-E, and select End Block.

Move to the second file with ALT-W, Open/Switch Window.

Move the cursor to the new location, and press ALT-W for the Window menu.

Move the block from the other window, press ALT-E, and select Hide/Show Block.

These commands move text from one window to another. You must open a window first (see Windows).

Optional Method to Move Text Within a File and Between Files (Versions 4.0 and 5.0)

CTRL Key Commands Delete the text to be moved, move to the new location, and use ^U (Unerase).

A quick method of moving text is to delete and restore it in a new location. ^U unerases text that has been deleted with one of the following commands:

^T	Deletes word
^Y	Deletes line
^QY	Deletes rest of line to right
^Q-DEL	Deletes rest of line to left
^KY	Deletes block

^U is limited to 500 characters (the limit of the unerase buffer). Use WSChange to increase the unerase buffer; however, a large buffer affects the memory available for editing. Unerase will not restore a single character deleted with ^G, ^H, DEL, or BACKSPACE. Unerase restores only the last deleted text.

NONDOCUMENT FILE

See Open a File and File Names.

NOTES (VERSION 5.0)

To Create a Note

CTRL Key Commands

^ONE	Onscreen, Note Endnote
^ONF	Onscreen, Note Footnote
^ONC	Onscreen, Note Comment
^ONI	Onscreen, Note Index Entry
^ONA	Onscreen, Note Annotation

Pull-Down Menu ALT-O (Other), Footnote/Endnote

To Set the Initial Value of a Note

Dot Command Use .F# *n* for a footnote and .E# *n* for an endnote. Substitute the starting number of the note for *n*.

To Edit a Note

CTRL Key Commands ^OND

Pull-Down Menu Use ALT-O (Other), Footnote/Endnote, D.

To Convert a Note from One Type to Another

CTRL Key Commands ^ONV

Pull-Down Menu Use ALT-O (Other), Footnote/Endnote, V.

Dot Command .CV *x*>*y*, where *x* equals the current note type (which does not include an index or annotation entry), and *y* equals the note type at print-time.

The dot command converts only when printing.

To Go to a Note

CTRL Key Commands Use ^ONG, indicate the type of note, and press F10.

Pull-Down Menu Use ALT-O (Other), Footnote/Endnote, G.

To Print Endnotes Other Than at the End of the Document

Dot Command .PE

To Spellcheck the Rest of the Notes

CTRL Key Commands ^ONL

Pull-Down Menu Use ALT-O (Other), Footnote/Endnote, L.

To Align Text in the Rest of the Notes

CTRL **Key Commands** ^ONU

Pull-Down Menu Use ALT-O (Other), Footnote/Endnote, U.

► OPEN A FILE

To Open a Document File At the Opening Menu

CTRL **Key Commands** Type **D** and a file name, and then press ENTER.

Pull-Down Menu Type **F** (File), and select Open a Document. Type a file name, and press ENTER.

Document files contain normal editing features, such as wordwrap, margins, and justification.

To Open a Nondocument File At the Opening Menu

CTRL **Key Commands** Type **N** and a file name, and then press ENTER.

Pull-Down Menu Type **F** and select Open a Nondocument File. Type a file name, and press ENTER.

Nondocument files are ASCII files without any formatting features. In a nondocument file you cannot center text, use hyphen help, justify text, use line spacing, set margins, or have wordwrap. Usually, nondocument files are used for programming or merge print data files.

Tab stops in nondocument files are set every eight spaces. Use ^OI to reset them to every 1, 2, 4, or 16 spaces. The page indicator in the status line does not exist in nondocument files. Use ^QI to find a page in a document file or a line in a nondocument file.

To change a file from a document file to a nondocument file, see ASCII Files. See also Starting WordStar.

OVERPRINT CHARACTERS

CTRL Key Commands Type the first character. Use ^PH (Print Controls menu, Overprint Char), and then type the second character.

Character Displayed "^H"

Overprint causes two characters to print in the same space. Use this to type foreign characters with accent marks. The two characters will not be overprinted on the screen. You may use ^P0 for foreign letters as well.

OVERPRINT LINES

CTRL Key Commands Type the first line. Use ^P-ENTER, and then type the second line.

Characters Displayed "-" (as a flag at the right of the screen)

Overprint causes two or more lines of text to be overprinted and is used when a line of text needs to be displayed with strike-out characters, usually for legal documents. One line contains the text, the second line a series of dashes or x's.

PAGE BREAK

Dot Command .PA

Pull-Down Menu ALT-L (Layout), New Page

Function Key ^F8

Characters Displayed "P" (as a flag)

Page breaks are automatically inserted every 55 lines by default. To insert a page break manually, use this command. Automatic page breaks can be changed on the screen by changing the Page Length command using .PL or by changing the top or bottom margin by using .MT or .MB.

PAGE LENGTH

Dot Command Use .PL *n*, where *n* equals lines. The default page length is 11 inches (normally 66 lines). For version 5, use *n*" to set in inches.

The Page Length command controls how long a page is and where page breaks occur. Top and bottom margins are subtracted from the specified page length to determine the page length on the screen. Because of that, the onscreen page length is usually less than the page length specified. To increase the page length on the screen, decrease the line height or the top and bottom margins.

PAGE NUMBERS

Dot Commands

.PN *n*	Prints page number, starting with page *n*
.PC *n*	Prints page number at column *n*
.OP	Omits page numbers
.PG	Prints page numbers (after .OP)

Pull-Down Menu ALT-L, Omit Page Numbering

The current page number displays at the top of the screen when editing a file, and prints centered at the bottom of each page. To change how the page number prints (except in a footer), use these dot commands.

To start the page number at a number other than 1, use .PN with a new number. To skip pages, turn off numbering with .OP on page 1, and start numbering with .PN at the top of the desired page. To stop printing page numbers entirely, use .OP. To resume printing page numbers after using .OP, use .PG or .PN followed by the page number. Use .PC*n* to place the page number across the page at a particular column number.

See Headers and Footers for more on page numbers.

PAGE OFFSET

See Margins.

PAGE PREVIEW (VERSION 5.0)

CTRL Key Commands ^OP (Onscreen, Page Preview)

Alternate Command ALT-1

Pull-Down Menu ALT-L (Layout), Page Preview

This command previews how a document will look when printed, including columns, headers, footers, footnotes, fonts, line spacing, and more. This feature only works with graphics monitors. Text cannot be edited in this mode.

To Display the Page in a Larger or Smaller View While in Page Preview

Pull-Down Menu In Page Preview, press ALT-V for the View menu, and select the desired view.

Alternate Command In Page Preview, type + to change to a larger view, and type - to change to a smaller view.

To Display a Grid Across the Page

Pull-Down Menu In Page Preview, press ALT-O for the Options menu, and select Grid.

To Go to a Page

Pull-Down Menu In Page Preview, press ALT-G for the Go To menu.

To Exit Page Preview

Command ESC

Alternate Command Press ALT-R to return to editing, and select Current Page or Original Page.

Alternate Command ALT-Z

PARAGRAPH MARGINS

See Margins.

PARAGRAPH NUMBERING (VERSION 5.0)

CTRL Key Commands Use ^OZ (Onscreen, Paragraph Number), and press ENTER to accept the number or letter, or press <Right> or <Left> to change the level.

Pull-Down Menu Press ALT-L for the Layout menu, and select Paragraph Numbering. Press ENTER to accept the number or letter, or press <Right> or <Left> to change the level.

This feature creates a dynamic numbering system that adjusts when paragraphs are added or deleted or when their order is changed. The numbering system can include Arabic numbers, Roman numerals, or letters, as in 2.2, II, ii, and A.1.a.

To Change the Starting Number From the Default of 1

Dot Command Use .P# *n*, where *n* represents the number to start with, such as 3 or 3.3.

To Change the Numbering System To Roman Numerals or Letters

Dot Command Use .P# *s*, where *s* represents the numbering system.

Substitute one or more of the following for *s*: Zoz for letters, 9 for numbers, I or i for Roman numerals. The command .P# Z.9.z will print the first paragraph (with a starting number of 1) with A.1.a.

To combine both a starting number and a numbering system, type the starting number first. For example, .P# 3.3.3, Z.9.z will produce C.3.c.

► PAUSE PRINTING

Before Printing

CTRL Key Commands ^PC (Print menu, Pause)

Character Displayed "^C"

This command is inserted before printing and temporarily halts the printer when a file is being printed. This is useful for inserting envelopes or changing print wheels or ribbons. When the printer is paused, the print screen will display "Print wait". (To view the printing screen, use ^P from the Opening menu or ^KP from within a document.) When you are ready to continue printing, type **C**. Type **B** afterwards to return to the Opening menu or to edit a document.

Alternatively, to cause the printer to pause between each page, type **Y** at the Pause Between Pages option when starting to print (see Printing).

When Printing

Opening Menu P (Print), P (Pause)

Pull-Down Menu F (File), P (Print), P (Pause)

To continue printing, type **C**.

► PHANTOM SPACE/PHANTOM RUBOUT

CTRL Key Commands Use ^PF (Print menu, Phantom Space) or ^PG (Print menu, Phantom Rubout).

Characters Displayed "^F" and "^G"

These commands allow you to print special characters that are not included on the standard keyboard, such as foreign letters or mathematical symbols. To change the default settings, use WSChange.

PITCH

CTRL Key Commands Use ^PN (Print menu, Normal Font) or ^PA (Print menu, Alternate Font).

Characters Displayed "^N" and "^A"

The default normal pitch (^PN) is 10 characters per inch (cpi). Change to alternate pitch (12 cpi) with ^PA. Use the Character Width command (.CW) to print other pitches available on your printer. To change the default pitch settings from 10 and 12 cpi, use WSChange. Do not use these commands with proportional printing in Version 5.0; use ^P= (Fonts).

PLACE MARKERS

To Set Place Marker

CTRL Key Commands Use ^K *n* (Block menu, Set Marker), where *n* equals marker number 0 through 9.

To Go to Place Marker

CTRL Key Commands Use ^Q *n* (for Quick menu, Marker), where *n* equals marker number 0 through 9.

This command allows you to set and quickly go to ten markers (0 through 9) in a file. It is useful for marking and finding special ruler lines, chapter headings, tables, and so on. Place markers must be set each time you open a file; they are not stored when you save a file. To delete a marker place the cursor next to it, use ^K, and type the marker number.

PRINTING

CTRL Key Commands At the Opening menu type **P**, or while editing use ^KP. Type in the file name. Edit options, if necessary, and press F10 for version 5.0, ESC for earlier versions. Alternatively, use ^PRTSCR to print.

Pull-Down Menu At the Opening menu type **F** (File), or while editing press ALT-F. Select Print a File, Edit options, if necessary, and press F10.

If you print the file being edited, the last saved version is printed and the current version cannot be saved until the printing is finished.

Print Options

Print Options	Default Setting
Page Numbers	All
All/Even/Odd Pages	All (version 5.0)
Printer Name	Installed default printer
Pause Between Pages	No
Use Form Feeds	No (Yes for laser printers)

Print Options	Default Setting
Nondocument	No (versions 4.0/5.0)
Number of Copies	1
Redirect Output To	None (version 5.0)

Page numbers can be specified as a range, such as 1 through 20, as individual pages, such as 1, 3, 6, or as a combination of both. To print odd or even pages, specify O or E.

To choose a printer, select from the list of printers displayed below the menu by typing the printer name or moving the cursor to the printer name. (Installed printers can be set up to print from alternate printer ports with WSChange.)

Commands to Use While Printing

The following commands can be used while printing:

P or ^KP	Displays Print menu
C	Continues after pause
B	Prints in background
F	Prints in foreground
P	Pauses printing
^U	Stops printing

▶ PROPORTIONAL SPACING

CTRL Key Commands Use ^P@ for proportionally spaced columns with version 5.0.

Dot Command .PS on or .PS off

Note: For version 5.0, use the Fonts command (^P=) for all proportional printing. Separate columns with tabs and make sure the margins and tabs are set in inches, not columns.

Use this command to print characters according to their relative widths. Proportional spacing does not display on the screen.

If columnar text, such as a table of numbers, does not print correctly, use ^P@ before each column on each line of the table. This will place the text in a particular column location.

► PROTECT A FILE (VERSIONS 4.0 AND 5.0)

CTRL Key Commands Type C at the Opening menu, and type in the file name.

Pull-Down Menu Type **F** (File) and type **C**

Type the file name and type **Y** to protect the file from inadvertent changes. You will be presented with limited menu choices and commands when viewing a protected file. Protect files when sharing disks or when using WordStar on a network. To unprotect, type **C** and the file name again.

QUIT

See Exit from a Menu and Exit from a Document.

READ A FILE

See Insert File.

RENAME A FILE

CTRL Key Commands At the Opening menu type **E**, or while editing use ^KE (Block menu, Rename), select the file to rename, and type the new file name.

Pull-Down Menu At the Opening menu type **F** (File), or while editing press ALT-F for the File menu, and select Rename a File. Select the file to rename and type the new file name.

This command gives a new name to a file. WordStar will not allow you to use a name that already exists or to rename a file that is being edited. The renamed file will always be located on the same drive and directory as the old.

REPEAT COMMAND

CTRL **Key Commands** Use ^QQ (Quick menu, Repeat), and type the character or command to be repeated.

The Repeat command repeats a single character or command. The command to be repeated can be a cursor movement or delete command, the Align command, or any other command displayed on the classic Edit menu. (You need not be using the classic menus.)

To stop the Repeat command, press any key except a number. To speed up or slow down the command, type a number from 0 through 9 (0 is the fastest, 9 is the slowest).

REPEAT PREVIOUS FILE NAME

CTRL **Key Commands** Use ^R when prompted for a file name.

Use this command any time WordStar prompts for a file name. It displays the file last edited, printed, or copied during the current WordStar session.

REPLACE

See Find/Replace Text.

RIGHT MARGIN

See Margins.

RULER LINE

To Insert or Change a Ruler Line (Versions 4.0 and 5.0)

CTRL Key Commands Use ^OO (Onscreen menu, Ruler Line). Inserts current ruler line at cursor position. As an option, you can edit the new ruler line.

Function Key Press F8. Inserts current ruler line above cursor in column 1. As an option, you can edit the new ruler line.

Dot Command Use .RR in column 1, and type in new ruler line.

To permanently imbed a ruler line in a file at the cursor location, use these commands. To change the margins and tab stops, type the margin or tab symbols listed here into the new ruler line. Text edited or aligned below the imbedded ruler line will conform to the new settings.

Symbol	What Is Edited
-	Ruler line
L	Left margin
R	Right margin
P	Paragraph margin
V	Temporary indent
!	Tab stop
#	Decimal tab stop

To Change the Current Ruler Line to Match Text (All Versions)

CTRL **Key Commands** Place the cursor on the line that contains the text. Use ^OF (Onscreen, Ruler from Text).

Use ^OF to temporarily set the current ruler line to match the margins of the text at the cursor location. For example, ^OF on a line of text that starts at column 10 will change the current left margin to 10.

To Turn the Ruler Line Display On or Off (All Versions)

CTRL **Key Commands** Use ^OT (Onscreen, Display On/Off).

The current ruler line is located above the text screen and below the menus. It displays the current left and right margins and tab stops.

RUN A PROGRAM OR DOS COMMAND

CTRL Key Commands At the Opening menu type **R**, or while editing (versions 4.0 and 5.0) use ^KF (Block menu, Run Program).

Pull-Down Menu At the Opening menu type **O** (for Other), or while editing press ALT-O (Other). Select Run a DOS command

This command will display the DOS prompt. Run DOS commands such as CHKDSK, FORMAT, or COPY, or run other programs depending on available memory. (Do not start memory-resident programs by using this command. Save and exit WordStar first.) After each program or command, WordStar will return to the Opening menu or the current document. To run a series of DOS commands without returning to WordStar, type **COMMAND** at the DOS prompt. To return to WordStar, type **EXIT** at the DOS prompt.

SAVE A FILE

To Save a File and Continue Editing

CTRL Key Commands Use ^KS (Block menu, Save and Resume).

Pull-Down Menu Press ALT-F for the File menu, and select Save File, Resume Editing.

Function Key F9

To Save and Exit a File

CTRL Key Commands Use the ^KD command (for Block menu, Save).

Pull-Down Menu Press ALT-F for the File menu, and select Save File, go to Opening screen.

Function Key F10

To Save a File and Exit to DOS

CTRL Key Commands Use ^KX (for Block menu, Save and Exit).

Pull-Down Menu Press ALT-F for the File menu, and select Save File, Exit WordStar.

To Save and Print a File (Accessing the Print Menu)

CTRL **Key Commands** Use ^KD (for Block menu, Save), and type **P** (Print). Type the file name and the options, and then press F10.

To Save and Print a File with Default Settings (Versions 4.0 and 5.0)

CTRL **Key Commands** ^PRTSC

To Save a File with a New Name (Version 5.0)

CTRL **Key Commands** Use ^KT (for Block menu, Save As), and type the file name.

Pull-Down Menu Press ALT-F for the File menu, and select Save and Name File. Type the file name and press ENTER.

To Save the Marked Block to a New File

CTRL **Key Commands** Mark the block. Use ^KW (Block menu, Write to Disk), and type the file name.

Pull-Down Menu Mark the block. ALT-E (Edit), write block to file. Type in name.

To Exit a File Without Saving (Abandon a File)

CTRL **Key Commands** Use ^KQ (for Block menu, Abandon Changes).

Pull-Down Menu ALT-F (File), Abandon Changes

Save a file when you are done editing unless changes are to be abandoned. Periodically save a file while you are editing. It is possible to have WordStar automatically and periodically save files. Use WSChange to turn on Auto-backup (see Automatic Backup.) This helps to prevent loss of data due to power loss, hardware failure, or user error. When a file is saved, the current version is copied to the disk. The last saved version is renamed with the same file name but a different extension (.BAK). To edit this file, rename it first with a different extension.

SCROLL SCREEN/TEXT

See the "Cursor Movement and Editing Commands" section of this book.

SHORTHAND (VERSIONS 4.0 AND 5.0)

To Define a Shorthand Character

Commands Press the ESCAPE key and type **?** to display or change definitions. Type a shorthand character, and type in a description. Press ENTER. Type in commands or characters, and press ENTER. Press ENTER to complete the command, and type **Y** to save changes to disk.

Shorthand assigns frequently used commands or keystrokes to a single shorthand character. The shorthand character can then be used to repeat the command or keystrokes while you edit any document. You can define 36 different shorthand characters: 26 letters and 10 digits. After defining a character, type in a description of the keystrokes to follow. This can be up to 50 characters long. Use it for remembering what the shorthand character does.

The characters or commands that are to be executed by the shorthand character must be typed exactly. You may use multiple lines. To use print control commands, precede each command with ^P. For instance, to enter a bold print control code (^PB), use ^PP^PB.

Save the changes to disk for permanent storage; otherwise, changes will be in effect only until you exit WordStar.

To Use Shorthand

Command Press ESC and type the shorthand character, or select a menu option.

For example, ESC-M executes a shorthand that types the word "MEMORANDUM". You may use the following options after the ESC key. Results or formulas are inserted from the last calculation with Calculator (^QM) or Block Math (^KM).

Option	Effect
^J or F1	Help
?	Displays and/or changes descriptions
@	Inserts today's date
!	Inserts the current time
=	Inserts results of the last calculation
$	Inserts formatted results
#	Inserts the formula of the last calculation

To increase the memory available for storing shorthand definitions, use WSChange.

SINGLE SPACE

See Line Spacing.

SOFT HYPHEN

To Turn the Display of Soft Hyphens Off or On

CTRL **Key Commands** Use ^OD (Onscreen menu, Display) or ^OP (Onscreen menu, Preview).

To Enter a Soft Hyphen

CTRL **Key Commands** Use the ^OE command (Onscreen, Soft Hyphen).

Soft hyphens are automatically inserted when you use hyphenation (see Hyphenation). To manually place a soft hyphen, move to the position in the word and use ^OE; an equal sign (=) will appear. A soft hyphen will print only when at the end of a line. Otherwise, it will be displayed as an equal sign (=) but will not print. In version 5.0, it disappears when in the middle of a paragraph. Use ^OD (Onscreen, Display) or ^OP (Onscreen, Preview) to turn the display of soft hyphens off and on.

SOFT SPACES

CTRL Key Commands Use ^OB to display the soft spaces as dots and ^OP to turn display off and on.

Soft spaces are automatically inserted between words when paragraphs are justified. They are deleted when the paragraph is realigned again without justification.

SOFT RETURNS (CONVERT TO)

CTRL Key Commands Use ^6 to convert hard returns to soft returns.

Soft returns occur at the end of the lines of a paragraph that has been aligned while typing or using ^B. They allow a paragraph to be realigned.

SORTING (VERSION 5.0)

To Sort Lines in Order of the Left Column

CTRL Key Commands Mark the block, and then use ^KZ.

This command sorts lines based on the left columns. Numbers are sorted after spaces and symbols but before letters.

To Sort Lines in Order of Columns Other Than the Left

CTRL **Key Commands** Use ^KN to turn on Column mode. Mark the columns to sort. Use ^KZ to sort.

For example, to sort lines located in columns 10 through 20, mark the beginning and end of columns when in Column mode.

SPEED WRITE (VERSION 5.0)

CTRL **Key Commands** Type an **S** at the Opening menu, and edit the file. When saving, type a file name.

Pull-Down Menu Type **F** at the Opening menu for the File menu, and edit the file. Save and type a file name.

Speed Write is a quick way of opening a file without first specifying a file name. If you have previously edited a file name, its name will be displayed.

SPELL CHECK

To Check the Word at the Current Cursor Location

CTRL Key Commands Place the cursor on the word to be checked. Use ^QN (Quick menu, Check Word), and select an option from the menu.

Pull-Down Menu Place the cursor on the word to be checked. Press ALT-O for the Other menu, and select Check Word Spelling. Select an option from the menu.

Function Key Place the cursor on the word to be checked. Press SHIFT-F4, and select an option from the menu.

To Check All Words After the Current Cursor Position

CTRL Key Commands Use ^QL (for Quick menu, Check Rest), and select an option from the menu.

Pull-Down Menu Use ALT-O (Other) and then select Check Document Spelling. Select an option.

Function Key Press SHIFT-F3 and select an option.

To Prompt for a Word to Check from the Keyboard

CTRL **Key Commands** Use ^QO (for Quick menu, Enter Word), and type in the word to be checked. Select an option from the menu.

The spelling corrector compares words in a file against words contained in dictionary files (MAIN.DCT and PERSONAL.DCT). When no match exists, the word is displayed along with suggested alternatives.

Here is a list of options:

- **I** ignores the selected word for the rest of the file and continues with the next word to check.
- **A** adds the selected word to the personal dictionary (PERSONAL.DCT). The word will be considered correctly spelled from then on.
- **B** bypasses the selected word this time only. It will be selected again if it exists in the file.
- **E** allows you to enter a replacement word from the keyboard.
- **G** globally replaces all instances of the selected word with the correction.

STARTING WORDSTAR

To Start WordStar and Go to the Opening Menu

Command Type **WS**.

To Start WordStar and Open a File

Command Type **WS** and the file name.

This command opens a file with the specified name in Document mode, unless the default has been changed with WSChange.

To Start WordStar and Open a Document File

Command Type **WS**, the file name, and then **D**.

To Start WordStar and Open a Nondocument File

Command Type **WS**, the file name, and then **N**.

To Start WordStar and Print a File

Command Type **WS**, the file name, and then **P**.

To Start WordStar, Print a File, and Exit

Command Type **WS**, the file name, and then **PX**.

► STRIKEOUT

CTRL **Key Commands** Move the cursor to the beginning of the text and use ^PX (Print menu, Strikeout).

Move the cursor to the end of the text and use ^PX.

Pull-Down Menu Move the cursor to the beginning of the text to be struck out, press ALT-S for the Style menu, and select Strikeout.

Move the cursor to the end of the text, press ALT-S for the Style menu, and select Strikeout.

Characters Displayed "^X"

Strikeout causes the printer to print a hyphen through text. Strikeout is highlighted on the screen. Use ^PX before and after the text to be struck out. To get rid of strikeout, delete the control characters. Turn the control character display off or on with ^OD. (See also Overprint Lines.)

To Redefine the Default Strikeout Character (-) (Version 5.0)

Dot Command Use .XX *letter*, where *letter* is the new strikeout character.

Type this command at the beginning of a file with the new strike out character. Use ^PX to activate the new character. Use WSChange to permanently change the default strikeout character.

► SUBSCRIPT

CTRL Key Commands Move the cursor to the start of the text to be included in the subscript, and use ^PV (Print menu, Subscript).

Move the cursor to the end of the text, and use ^PV.

Pull-Down Menu Move the cursor to the start of the text to be included in the subscript, press ALT-S for the Style menu, and select Subscript.

Move the cursor to the end of the text, press ALT-S for the Style menu, and select Subscript.

Characters Displayed "^V"

When typed before and after text, Subscript prints text below the rest of the text on the line, as in H_2O. Subscripted text is highlighted on the screen. To get rid of subscripting, delete the control characters. Turn the control character display off or on with ^OD.

Normally, the printer will roll down 3/48 inch. To change this, use the dot command .SR *n* on a line above the text to be subscripted, where *n* is in 48ths of an inch; for example, .SR 4 is a subscript roll of 4/48 inch.

SUPERSCRIPT

CTRL Key Commands Move the cursor to the start of the text to be included in the superscript, and use ^PT (Print menu, Superscript).

Move cursor to the end of the text and use ^PT.

Pull-Down Menu Move the cursor to the start of the text to be included in the superscript, press ALT-S for the Style menu, and select Superscript.

Move the cursor to the end of the text, press ALT-S for the Style menu, and select Superscript.

Characters Displayed "^T"

When typed before and after text, Superscript prints text above the rest of the text on the line, as in 10^2. Superscripted text is highlighted on the screen. To get rid of superscripting, delete the control characters. Turn the control character display off or on with ^OD.

Normally, the printer will roll up 3/48 inch. To change this, use the dot command .SR *n* above the text to be superscripted, where *n* is in 48ths of an inch; for example, .SR 4 is a superscript roll of 4/48 inch.

TABLE OF CONTENTS

To Create Table of Contents Entries

Dot Command .TC *text* ... #, where *text* is the entry and # is the page-number symbol that WordStar will replace.

Pull-Down Menu ALT-O (Other), Table of Contents entry

On the first page of each new section of text, create a line that contains the table of contents entry; for example:

```
.TC WORDSTAR COMMANDS .... 20
```

Place the dot command in column 1. When the table of contents is created, the correct page number will replace the # symbol. To create levels of entries, indent the text with spaces; for example:

```
.TC             Table of Contents Entries ... 36
```

To Create the Table of Contents (From the Opening Menu)

Classic Menu Type **T** at the Opening menu. Type the file name and the range of pages, or type **O** for Odd or **E** for Even. Press F10 to start for version 5.0, ENTER for earlier versions..

Pull-Down Menu Type **O** for the Other menu, and select Table of Contents. Type the range of pages, or type **O** for Odd or **E** for Even, or press F10 to start.

A separate file with the extension .TOC and the file name of the document file will be created. Edit and print this as the table of contents.

Create a separate table of contents for the same document by substituting the dot command .TC1 for .TC at different entries. A separate file with the appropriate extension will be created. Numbers 1 through 9 can be used in the dot command to create up to nine separate files.

► TABS

To Change Tab Settings

CTRL Key Commands Use ^OI, add or delete numbers, and press F10.

Pull-Down Menu Press ALT-L for the Layout menu, and select Margins and Tabs. Move to the Tabs field and add or delete numbers, and press F10.

Dot Command .TB *n* or *n*"

Tab stops are displayed in the ruler line as exclamation points (!). When editing a document, press the TAB key to move the cursor to the next tab stop to the right.

The CTRL key and pull-down menu commands display the Margins and Tabs menu. Add or delete the tab settings here. Settings are in inches except for .TB*n*. Press F10 when the command is complete; tab settings are stored in the file with .TB.

The new tab settings will be in effect for all text that follows. When setting multiple tab stops, separate each number with spaces or commas.

(See Ruler Line for more on using .RR. See also Decimal Tabs).

► UNDERLINE

CTRL Key Commands Move the cursor to the beginning of the text, and use ^PS (Print menu, Underline).

Move the cursor to the end of the text, and use ^PS.

Pull-Down Menu Move the cursor to the beginning of the text, press ALT-S for the Style menu, and select Underline.

Move the cursor to the end of the text, press ALT-S for the Style menu, and select Underline.

Function Key Move the cursor to the beginning of the text, and press F3.

Move the cursor to the end of the text, and press F3.

Characters Displayed "^S"

When placed before and after text, this command causes text to be printed with an underline. Text is underlined and highlighted on the screen. To remove underlining, delete the control characters before and after the text. Display or turn off the underlining control characters with ^OD.

UNDO/UNERASE (VERSIONS 4.0 AND 5.0)

CTRL Key Commands ^U

Use this command to do the following:

- Restore the last deleted text, up to 500 characters

- Move text by restoring deleted text to a new location
- Exit a classic menu
- Stop printing
- Stop commands such as Find and Replace
- Exit the spelling corrector and Thesaurus
- Turn off hyphenation for the current paragraph

Unerase will not restore more than 500 characters at a time, unless the buffer size is increased with WS-Change. If a buffer is exceeded, a warning message will appear. If you type **Y** to continue, only part of the deleted text can be restored.

Single characters deleted with ^G, ^H, BACKSPACE, or DEL cannot be restored unless you customize the default settings with WSChange.

► WINDOWS (VERSION 5.0)

To Open or Switch to a Window

CTRL **Key Commands** Use the ^OK command (for Onscreen, Open/Switch Window). Type in the name of the file, and press ENTER.

Pull-Down Menu Press ALT-W for the Window menu, and select Open/Switch Between Windows. Type in the name of the file and press ENTER.

This command allows two files to be displayed and edited simultaneouly. The screen is divided into window 1 and window 2. Use ^OK to switch back and forth between them. To exit one of the files, switch to that window and use ^KD to save any changes or ^KQ to abandon the file.

To Size a Window

CTRL Key Commands Switch to the window to be sized and use ^OM (Window, Size Current Window). Type in the number of lines to display, and press ENTER.

Pull-Down Menu Press ALT-W to get to the Window menu, and select Size Current Window. Type in the name of the file, and press ENTER.

Use this command to control the number of lines that a window takes up on the screen. Press ENTER or type **0** to display each window as a full screen and to switch to the other window.

WINSTALL/WSCHANGE

These contain programs for setting up WordStar to work with your monitor and printer and to change default settings. Consult the WordStar manual.

WORD WRAP

CTRL **Key Commands** Use ^OW (Onscreen, Word Wrap Off/On).

This command turns Word Wrap off or on. Wordwrap causes text at the end of a line to move to the next line.

WRITING TO A FILE

See Copy Text.